MW00679609

LIFE
Before and After
DEATH

True Stories

By Betty R. Hatter

Heart to Heart Publishing, Inc.

Heart to Heart Publishing, Inc.
528 Mud Creek Road • Morgantown, KY 42261
(270) 526-5589
www.hearttoheartpublishinginc.com

Copyright © 2017
Publishing Rights: Heart to Heart Publishing, Inc.
Publishing Date February 14, 2018
Library of Congress Control Number: 2017957754
ISBN 978-1-937008-60-4

Author: Betty R. Hatter
Senior Editor and Cover Photography: L.J. Gill
Editor: Nicki Bishop
Designer: April Yingling-Jernigan

First Edition
10 9 8 7 6 5 4 3 2

Heart to Heart Publishing, Inc. books are available at a special discount for
bulk purchases in the US by corporations, institutions and other organizations.
For more information, please contact Special Sales at 270-526-5589.

Foreword

Being the pastor of a church has its share of both challenges and rewards. In the four churches where I've had the opportunity to serve, I have always considered the relationships my family and I have made to be one of the greatest rewards. Even though pastors do their best to minister to everyone equally, it is inevitable that we develop stronger relationships with certain members. Betty Ruth Hatter is one of those special people the Lord brought into my life when I became Pastor of Sulphur Spring Baptist Church in Franklin, Kentucky. There were times we laughed together, and there were times we cried together.

I will never forget the tremendous amount of faith she displayed when both her daughter Nancy and her husband Jimmy died within just a few months of one another. When I visited with her, following Jimmy's death, it only took a few moments for Betty Ruth to remind me that her faith was unshakeable. She shared with me that she didn't want Jimmy's funeral to be a wake. Instead, she wanted it to be a celebration.

So that's what we did! We told stories, we laughed, we celebrated the opportunity we had to know and love Jimmy, and then we worshipped our Lord by singing and praising the name of Jesus. It was a celebration, not only of the life Jimmy lived, but also of the fact he was now walking the streets of gold with his Lord and Savior Jesus Christ.

Betty Ruth Hatter is an amazing and well-respected woman. Her legacy as a wife, mother, grandmother and great-grandmother is strong. However, in my humble opinion, her Christian faith and her commitment to the Lord is undeniably her greatest quality. I'm confident you will enjoy reading this book and learning more about the amazing woman I am privileged to call my friend.

~ Rev. Matthew A. Sickling
Director of Missions, Ohio County Baptist Association
Pastor, Sulphur Spring Baptist Church, 1998-2009

Betty Ruth McCarroll about 6 months old

What a Morning?

It was the morning of March 30, 2012. Ready early for my hair appointment, I decided to start packing for my trip the next day. I would fly from Nashville to the Greenville-Spartanburg airport where Elaine and Ron were to meet me. After packing some things, I realized I didn't feel well. There wasn't any pain, I just didn't feel right. Sitting down in my recliner didn't ease the discomfort, so my last thought was to try a Coca Cola. If that didn't help, nothing would.

The only problem was I couldn't stand up. Easing myself to the floor to keep from falling, I reached for my phone. First, I dialed a dear friend, but there was no answer. Lying in the floor, I remembered that my son-in-law,

Ron, was at home, so I called him. Thankful he answered, I told him what was happening. I was going to call 911, and that's just what I did. I dialed what I thought was Franklin's 911 and gave them my information, but once again I was in for a surprise. They told me they didn't have a street by that name. I had to explain where I was to the 911 operator of the city of Bowling Green.

The ambulance soon arrived, and I told the EMT how to get into the house. Another problem—they couldn't get in. So, I dragged myself on the floor and reached the door to open it. Emergency workers put me on the cot and loaded me in the ambulance. I heard the paramedic tell the EMT driver that he needed to get a move on. I don't remember anything after we left my short driveway. There was one last problem to reckon with. My heart had stopped.

Let me go back to the very beginning. I was born at home in Robertson County, Tennessee, January 11, 1931. My dad was a sharecropper who worked hard, but that was during the time of the Great Depression.

I never knew we were poor, because most everyone else was too.

Sonny Boy

One of my favorite stories my dad used to tell was about an early recollection at church. When he was a young boy, his church got together and prepared a "Children's Day." On Sunday morning, all of the children lined up in front of the church. The visiting pastor came forward and began asking each one a question.

He went down the line and asked one little boy, "Sonny Boy, who made you?"

The boy answered, "The dust of the earth." The pastor asked again, and the boy gave the same answer.

The pastor finally said, "No, Sonny Boy. God made you."

The boy answered, "No. The boy God made tore his britches and had to go home."

She'd Do
It Again

This morning, I was reminded of another story that has passed down through the years. Mother had two older sisters and one younger. She and her younger sister usually played well together, but not this time. Mother had her own little ceramic iron, probably a Christmas gift. One day, as she played with it, Aunt Tommie grabbed the iron away from Mother and took off running around the house. As they neared the front porch, Aunt Tommie threw the iron onto the porch and it shattered into pieces. Mother caught her just as they reached a rose bush. She shoved her sister into the rose bush, while Mama Harris sat sewing in the yard. As Mother passed, Mama swatted at her and her sewing thimble went flying through the air. They never found the thimble, and Mother wasn't sorry for it. In fact, if Mother were living today, she would tell you that she would do it all over again. Her sister should have left her iron alone!

Ed and Annie Harris McCarroll on their wedding day

Over the Fence Courtship

Mother often helped her dad with the farm work while my dad worked the farm across the fence. Papa would always tell my Mother to stop looking at that young man and get back to doing what she was supposed to do. The day that Mother and Daddy were married was a surprise for the family. Mother was still in school.

That morning, Daddy had an automobile accident—he had somehow turned over his car. He was close to Mama and Papa's house when it happened. So, Mama wet a washcloth and cleaned his head where he had bumped it. Mother always said that Mama Harris would have put a knot on the other side of his head if she had known what was about to take place. People said that they ran away and got married. Mother said they didn't run, but they were almost caught. They were married for forty-seven years before Dad's death.

Daddy

My parents and I moved to Springfield when I was about twelve. Daddy started out working for a grocery store. We later moved to Franklin, KY, where he was meat manager of the A&P store. Before we left Springfield, Daddy was drafted to be part of the armed forces of World War II. They checked him and thought he was drunk. I never knew my daddy to take a drink.

They had him to sit in an open window for forty-five minutes and then examined him again. They determined that he had a heart murmur. It had probably been there all his life. Mother was very happy to hear that he did not pass, but she was very worried because they had found something wrong.

Daddy worked very hard, and he played just as hard. I found a picture of him on the Pleasant View High School basketball team. He could play horseshoes all day long. He and Mother made a croquet yard behind their house, lights and all. Several members of the Franklin-Simpson boys' basketball team learned to play in our backyard with Daddy as their helper.

Our weekly paper publishes a "50 years ago" page. The August 6, 1996 issue included a segment of the August 6,1946 issue. In 1946, there was a baseball league in Franklin. They gave the statistics for the top ten batters. A young man (I think he was 18 years old) and my dad (age 39) were tied for the top with a batting average of 563. Daddy also liked to fish, play Rook, etc.

He used to tell about seeing Babe Ruth playing ball. Babe Ruth was playing in a Nashville exhibition game in 1926. I never thought to ask him how he knew that Babe Ruth would be playing in Nashville. I remember when I was a little girl, there would be posters on fence posts or the sides of barns, maybe even trees. I'm very sure that he didn't have a radio in those days, but in some way word got around.

There is a note in the Simpson County history that my dad helped to organize a Sunday School at a new mission named Walker Avenue. That mission became Calvary Baptist Church.

After my children were born and continuing to my grand children, we called him Daddy Ed. He would be so proud of his great-grandchildren if he had lived to see them grow up.

His health started failing in 1973. He was in and out of hospitals for several months. They ran lots of tests. Mama Harris (my grandmother) died in January of 1975, but he was not well enough to go to Springfield for the funeral. From then on he had good days and not so good days.

Jameson (Elaine's son) was born in March of 1975. For some reason, Daddy Ed had in his head that Jameson was not going to live. Finally, one day he thought he could ride to Sligo, KY to see Jameson. We made the trip fine. He saw Jameson and then he knew the things he had been thinking were not true. All the way home to Franklin, he sang the song,

"Ready to go, Ready to stay,
Ready my place to fill.
Ready for service lowly or great,
Ready to do His will."

On May 30th, he went to Kentucky Lake
to go fishing with my husband, Jimmy, and
my Uncle Johnnie. At one time, they had to
go to the bank and let him out of the boat.
He rested there in the grass. The Fourth of
July, the family came to Mother and Daddy's
house. He spent part of the day pitching
horse shoes. He probably won. He didn't
have much energy after that day. Daddy
had multiple myeloma, cancer of the bone
marrow. He died August 5, 1975. We used
the song "Ready" at his funeral.

Mother

Mother was always beside Dad in whatever he did. She helped in the fields while they were farming. For years, she did the laundry in a zinc tub with clothes being scrubbed on a washboard. When we moved off the farm into Springfield, my sister was young and she needed attention. Of course, I was in need of some attention also. I am sure that we kept her busy.

When we moved into Kentucky, Mother soon got a part time job. It led to a full-time job. Mother taught three-year-olds in Sunday School for thirty-four years. She sang in the church choir for fifty plus years. She loved to play croquet as much as anyone and won as many games as anyone. She talked about riding a horse to church when she was young. I believe if she had been born at another time, she could have made the Olympics.

After Mother retired, she started taking care of school teachers' children. When school was out because of snow, she would go with my husband, Jimmy, on the mail route.

Mother died July 29, 2004 from a stroke, after a long battle with breast cancer. She drove a great grandson to school every morning during the month of April, prior to her death.

Mother was known as Bubba by her grandchildren, great-grandchildren and a lot of the people in the county. She didn't want to be called "Grandmother."

Betty Ruth at 6 years old

Bashful Me

I don't remember much about those early years, but Mother did tell a story or two about me. The children were supposed to sing at church one Sunday morning. I was younger than the rest. When Sunday came, I would not walk up front. Instead, I stood on the pew with my arm around Mother's neck and sang every word of the song.

I remember going to a family reunion every year for a while. I don't know whose family it was. They didn't have our last name. They always had goat barbeque and what they called dressed bananas. I don't remember eating the barbeque, but I still like dressed bananas. After lunch, they would tell Mother to have me stand on the front porch.

That was to be the stage where they wanted me to sing. I remember I always sang, "Jesus Loves Me".

One Room School

Daddy was a sharecropper. The farm owner's daughter was a school teacher. The year I was five, there weren't enough students to keep the one-room school open. I wouldn't be six until January. The teacher came up with the idea that if the school board would let me go to school, she would give me a ride each day. So, that's what happened. I don't remember much about school that year, but I do remember a young boy, probably in the eighth grade. He played the fiddle at the Grand Ole Opry for years.

I do remember the Christmas program. There was an old pump organ in the building. Someone played it as my mother sang, "It Came Upon the Midnight Clear." I heard

Mother sing a lot, but that's the only time I ever heard her sing a solo in public. She was in the church choir for over fifty years after we moved to Kentucky. We sang as we did the dishes at home. On the way home from the Christmas program that evening, I can remember as if it were yesterday. I spoke up and said "You know what? Santa Claus had on shoes just like Daddy's." It was probably three or four more years before I knew why.

After that year, the one room school must have closed, because I went to Cedar Hill School in second grade. Cedar Hill had twelve grades. Since I have begun writing, here are the little things I remember about school in those days:

* I remember some of the boys' and girls' names in my grade.

*I remember how, every November first, the school's outhouses (one girl's and one boy's) were turned over on Halloween night.

*I remember being in a Christmas play in the fifth grade. I had to have a pair of pajamas to wear, probably the first pajamas I ever had.

In the play, I was to strike a match and light a candle. I got up in front of everyone, struck the match, lit the candle; and then I blew out both the match and candle in one breath! Thankfully, I got a second chance, and that time I did it!

Cod Liver Oil

As a child, I was very thin. I have told people that I grew up in Tennessee and grew out in Kentucky. At some point in my childhood, someone decided that I needed cod liver oil. My tummy didn't think so. When Mother would pour a spoonful and put it in my mouth, I would swallow it and then it would come back up. Daddy wasn't always in the house when she gave it to me, but when he was, he would complain about my response.

He was in the house one day when Mother gave me a spoonful. It came back up, as always. Of course, Daddy complained again. While he was complaining, Mother poured another spoonful and popped it in his mouth. The cod liver oil affected him worse than it did me. Daddy took the bottle and he went out the back door. There was a sinkhole several yards behind the house. He didn't stop until he was close enough to throw that bottle right into the hole. No More Cod Liver Oil!!!

Tobacco Worm Soup

Growing up on a farm, the main crop was tobacco. Lots of times, Mother and I would go to the field with Daddy. We would probably walk a mile and had to cross a deep gully with a foot-log across it. Daddy was always talking about how good tobacco worm soup was. There came a time when Mother had heard him say it one too many times. That day she gave me a tobacco leaf. I was to walk beside her, and when she found a worm she would place it on the leaf.

It became time to go to lunch. Mother took the tobacco leaf, and the three of us started to the house. Daddy offered to carry the leaf, especially just before we crossed the gully. Mother knew what he intended to do so she did not let him take control. We made our way to the house, and as Mother was putting the meal on the table she included the worms on a syrup can top. I don't remember whether the worms were moving on the top or if she had beheaded them in the field. Either way, they were gross, disgusting and sickening. I remember Daddy begging, "Mother, please don't make me eat those worms and I'll never mention tobacco worm soup again." She let him plead a little while before removing the worms. Daddy kept his word.

Uncle Tom Dick

This story was told about Mother's oldest sister. Someone had called their uncle by name--I think it was Thomas Jefferson Davis. That was not what my Aunt Frances heard. It struck her funny bone. She spoke up and said, "Now isn't he a funny Uncle Tom Dick?" It stuck. That is the only name I ever heard him called.

I remember him, and I remember a story that he told. He was a carpenter by trade, and at the time of the story, he lived in a boarding house in Wheeling, West Virginia. He needed to go to the bathroom, and the door was unlocked. So, he opened the door and went in. There was a woman in the bathtub! She jumped up and screamed and put a washcloth over her face. I heard him tell the story a few times, and he still thought it was funny.

There is a beautiful piece of furniture in my home that he made. It is called a smoking stand, but in my home it's used as a telephone stand. I hope the piece can be passed down in my family. No one else in the family remembers either him or the stories.

Betty Ruth and Shirley Ann McCarroll

Baby Sister

I had a baby sister born November 7, 1941. Her name is Shirley Ann. She grew up to be a science teacher, mostly for sixth graders. She also worked for NASA, and she loved the rockets. I had new neighbors, so I carried some food over to welcome them to the neighborhood. As we talked about what we might have in common, one young man learned that I was "Miss Shirley's" sister. He was excited, "Miss Shirley taught us about rockets and let us shoot them."

Unfortunately, the rocket launches had to be stopped after a while. She taught for thirty-eight years before retiring. Now, she lives in an assisted living home. She has three daughters, two grandsons and two granddaughters, one great-granddaughter and one great-grandson.

Watching the Trains

The year was 1942, and there was a blackberry patch close to the railroad track near our house. Blackberries were especially nice that year. As they ripened, Mother and I would pick them. Mother would make fresh blackberry cobblers and jam for us to have for winter.

The first day and every day we picked, trains would come along the tracks. They were filled with soldiers either changing camps or on their way to be deployed. Mother and I would stand and wave at them until the train had passed. I can still remember seeing the soldiers, all dressed alike, waving at us. The trains were traveling past Cedar Hill, Tennessee toward Springfield, Tennessee then on to Nashville, Tennessee and beyond. The troops may have left from Fort Campbell, but I didn't know for sure.

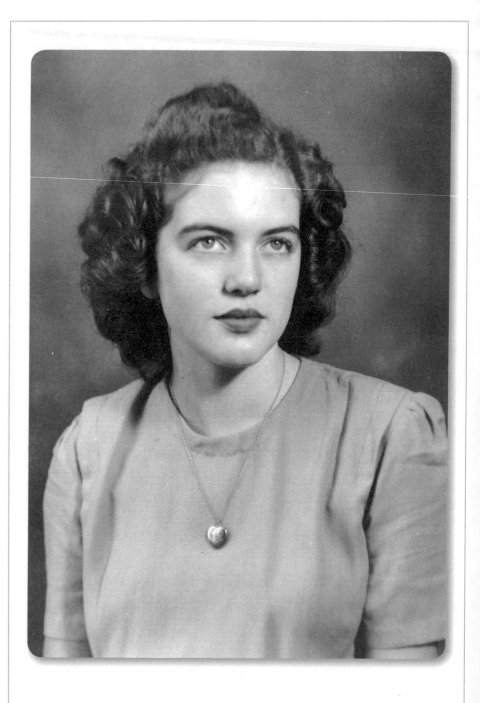

From Tennessee to Kentucky

When Daddy was transferred to Franklin, Kentucky, I had to stay in Springfield, Tennessee for five months and finish the ninth grade. I was taking Latin and the course was not offered at Franklin-Simpson High School. I stayed with my maternal grandparents, Papa and Mama Harris. Each Friday afternoon I would board a Greyhound bus and travel to Goodlettsville, Tennessee, transfer to another bus and end up in Franklin. On Sunday afternoon Mother and Daddy would then take me back to Springfield. Attending church in Franklin on Sunday mornings gave me the chance to meet people. This included some of my future classmates which helped me to make the transition into my new town. Mother said that she cried when they went over the Tennessee/Kentucky state line. Later, she said that she would have cried if she had to move back to Tennessee. As for me, the move was the beginning of a new and exciting chapter in my life.

Jimmy Hatter in 1943

Jimmy

Jimmy, my husband to be, was born December 5, 1924 in a farmhouse in Simpson County, KY. He had an older sister, Lucy, who passed away August 5, 2015. Jimmy's mother told me one day that she heard a frantic call, "Mother, come get me!" When she went outside to see what the trouble was, she saw a 2 year old boy sitting on the cone of the house. Someone had put the ladder up against the back of the house. Somehow, she was able to coax him to come down.

He used his straw hat as his steering wheel. Around the hillside, he would steer with his straw hat, delivering the mail like Mr. Denver, according to Jimmy. He probably never thought about having the opportunity to be a mail carrier.

There are some pictures with several sheep with him. As a member of the Future Farmers of America, the sheep must have been his project.

Jimmy missed a year of school in grade school because of illness. In the eleventh grade, he became eighteen years old in December, 1942. He was called to serve in the army, March of his Junior year. He received his basic training in Louisiana, then was sent to New Jersey for radio training. From there his assignment was in Europe, where he served as the radio man in the Captain's tank. A hand grenade was thrown into his tank, injuring the Captain and Jimmy. When D-Day happened, if I remember, he was in Wales.

After serving thirty-three months, he was discharged at Christmas time. Arrangements were made for him to go back to school, graduating in 1946. Each day of that semester, I saw him in the library. I don't think he saw me. He was seated with six girls.

Wedding day, 1949

Marriage

Jimmy and I were married January 29, 1949. We lived with his parents, and I gave birth to two daughters twenty-eight months apart. We named them Nancy and Elaine. In the spring of 1952, a farm in the neighborhood was put on the market. It went up for auction. Jimmy went to the auction but didn't buy it. The next day the family came to us, begging us to buy it. We bought forty acres for $9,300. (In the fall of 2015, a farm two miles away brought $6,500 an acre.)

There was an old house on the forty acres. They had papered and painted to make the house look better. The summer was very hot. Wallpaper had been placed on the top of ceiling planks on the walls. As the summer grew hotter, the wallpaper would burst between the cracks on the walls. It sounded like we were being shot.

The cold winter brought challenges also. The house wasn't underpinned. The fish froze in the fish bowl, sitting on the hearth with fire in the grate.

Someone asked me, "Did the fish thaw?"

I said, "No, they didn't want to freeze again."

The kitchen floor was covered with linoleum. When the wind blew, the linoleum rug in the kitchen would rise about eight inches off the floor. Thankfully, by the next summer, the wallpaper had been redone and the house had been underpinned.

In the years that followed, little by little, bit by bit, we made a very nice place to live. It had two extra bedrooms upstairs, insulation, heat and air, county water and a full bath. When we moved in, we had four rooms and a path to the outhouse.

Nancy had seven bad teeth in her mouth. I had taken her to the dentist. He said, "Leave them alone. They will come out on their own." We learned that Nancy was diabetic when she was seven years old. The first thing they did was to pull those same teeth. Nancy had her ups and downs, but on the whole she was OK. She graduated high school with honors and earned her Bachelor's degree from Western Kentucky University in Bowling Green, Kentucky. She went to the mission field all three summers, taught first grade in our school system and went to WKU for her Master's. She married December 18, 1976, and had two sons. She also continued teaching.

Nancy often taught the Children's Sermon portion at our church. Not only could she captivate the attention of children of every age, the adults would sit on the edge of their seats hanging on every word. She led a children's choir at church. They sang at her wedding. She sang in the adult church choir.

She became iffy with her husband but didn't leave him immediately. She informed him that he had to pay the bills. She did leave him when it became too much strain. She was going to school to earn her Doctor of Early Childhood Education degree. With help from her daddy and I, she received her doctorate from Nova Southeastern University. She went to Argentina to teach the missionaries' children while they were having some special classes. She left on Christmas Eve, 1999. In March 2001, she became sick and passed away eight days later with pneumonia. What a shock to the family, her school, our church and the community. She was fifty-one years old.

All three girls were, and still are, very special. Elaine has the voice of an angel. (More than her mom would tell you that.) She was an honor student, attended Western Kentucky University, and she married a young man she met at WKU. He became a pastor when he was nineteen. After several years he earned his Master's Degree and

later completed his Ph.D. in New Testament. He taught in the Religion Department at Gardner-Webb University in Boiling Springs, NC.) Elaine received her Master's the same day her youngest son received his. She served as a guidance counselor at a high school. They have recently moved to Owensboro, Ky (because of her husband's health).

Marla came along ten plus years after Elaine. That may be the biggest laugh of all. She tells people that she is an only child with two sisters. Marla sings very, very well, but she is known for playing the piano. She was also an honor student and has been married to Michael Jordan for over thirty years. She graduated from WKU with a Bachelor of Science Degree in Computer Science and her husband has his Undergraduate Degree from WKU with his Master's in Special Education from the University of Louisville. Michael taught public school for twenty-five years, and, due to health issues, had to retire. Marla has worked over thirty years in the IT industry. They have a son, Bryan, and a daughter, Christa. They currently live in Louisville.

Farm life in 1949

Shelling Peas

In the fifties, my sister-in-law and I were trying to do a good deed. Our neighbor was in the hospital. Someone told us she had peas that needed to be taken care of. I don't remember who picked them, but Lucy and I were intending to shell them. I had heard that you could shell peas with the washing machine wringer...and you can. We placed a clean white sheet in the bottom of the washing machine to keep everything sanitary. We began!!

I told you that you could shell the peas with the washing machine wringer. I didn't tell you to WATCH OUT! The peas in the hulls did not go through the wringer. The hulls went out on the other side, but the peas came back at us like bullets. They zipped by and didn't land in the washing machine. We were thankful that we hadn't sent but two or three hulls through the first time. The floor was swept, the birds outside were fed and we started all over again. This time, one of us kept the hulls going through, the other one used a cookie sheet and banked the peas into the washer onto the clean cloth.

When we were finished, I don't know what happened to the peas. I didn't cook them, can them, or freeze them. Maybe Lucy did.

Betty Ruth with Elaine and Nancy

Children Helping

Sometimes, we worked together as a family. When Nancy was seven and Elaine was five, we went to chop out tobacco. We started on our rows. Elaine was chopping out tobacco. To Jimmy and I that meant to chop out the weeds, but to Elaine it meant chopping out every tobacco plant she came to. You may think she was punished in some way. She wasn't. She was doing exactly what she had been told to do.

Nancy and Elaine rode the tobacco setter when they were a little older. They not only did our farm but three or four neighboring farms. They had such good rhythm that they missed placing very few plants in the mechanism of the tobacco setter. They sang a lot to keep the beat, and they didn't consider it work.

The End of the World

It was a beautiful morning. We had a garden planted on a plot away from the farm where we lived. The garden had some vegetables that needed to be picked. Mother came to help me or maybe it was for me to help her. The girls were staying at our house. Mother and I were busy, when all of a sudden there was a loud BOOM.

I started running across the field headed for our house. Mother called to me, "Come back, we have my car." We started toward the house and met Nancy driving our car. Although she wasn't old enough to drive legally, she had told Elaine and Marla to get into the car. They were coming to see if Bubba and I were alright. The loud BOOM was the natural gas line exploding. It was less than a mile from the house. We lived on that farm for fifty years. It was the only time the line exploded. We thought that it could be the end of the world!!!

Marla around 1965

Isn't it Pretty?

The post on our front porch had just been painted with a fresh coat of clean, WHITE paint. Marla was about 5 years old. She came to get me so I could see what she had done.

As we went to the front porch, her remark was, "See, isn't it pretty?"

My reply was, "NO!!!" She had made some red clay mud, packed the posts about ten inches high with her handiwork. About the same time, her Dad came into sight, coming down the road on the tractor. I told Marla that she had better get that mud off before her Dad got to the house. There was no way. She removed the red clay mud, but the post had a pink tint for a long time.

She will still tell you, "It was pretty".

Vacation Time

    As we left home, Marla and I had no idea where we were going. Jimmy had told us we were going on vacation and let us know the time we would be leaving. He must have told us how long we would be gone. We packed clothes we hoped were appropriate, and we were on our way.

    The bank was not open as we went through town. Marla and I wondered about the money. Jimmy drove south on 31-W, turned onto Hwy 109 and drove east on I-40. We stopped at a rest area after Crossville, and there was an advertisement for "The Music Man" being performed at the Crossville Theater. Marla and I wished we could see it. Jimmy made reservations for us the night that we would come back through. We traveled on… our destination was Gatlinburg.

For the first morning's breakfast, Marla ordered half a cantaloupe. It fed all three of us, it was so large. It was a breakfast to remember. That day, we went to the place that is now Dollywood. Jimmy could have watched the blacksmith work all day.

The next day, we enjoyed the beautiful scenery of the mountains with a trip to the water show that evening. The water show was a sight to see, but there is another memory that we haven't forgotten. A young boy, about fifteen years old, was selling chocolate-covered, frozen bananas. He was the best salesman I have seen, before or after. I've often wondered what happened to that young man. I hope he still has the enthusiasm for work and life as he had then.

The next morning, we drove beside the stream and up the mountain. The water was clear and inviting. Jimmy found a place to park, then he and Marla made their way to the stream. Just as Jimmy stepped into the water,
I said, "Jimmy, be careful. That's your last pair of clean pants." Too late, he had slipped

on a rock before I finished telling him.

Later in the day, we drove to Crossville, found a motel room for the night and went to see "The Music Man." It was a night of enjoyment!

We left for home the following morning. Marla and I had not spent a penny. We wonder, even now, where Jimmy had all the twenty-dollar bills stashed that we saw him take out of his pockets. A great time was had by all.

Funerals

I sang for funerals. Sometimes, the families asked for me, and other times the funeral home called and asked if I was available. There was a need when Marla was about six months old. Jimmy was busy, and the girls were in school. My mother-in-law was working, but she said she could leave early and she would take care of Marla. The time arrived—no mother-in-law.

At the time, the piano was in the front of the funeral home. There was a floor lamp on each end of the piano. Marla sat in my lap for me to sing. She took a hold of the floor lamp close to us and shook it the whole time that I was singing. From that time until now, Marla has always found something funny at the funeral home. When she was able to drive to school, I would tell her that if school became too boring, go to the funeral home and stay thirty minutes and then go back to school.

As I was writing this, it came to my mind that maybe the humor she found at funeral homes was inherited. Mother and I were going to visit "Miss Betty," the lady for whom I was named. I was six or seven at the time. When we arrived, "Miss Betty" was preparing to go to a funeral. She wanted us to go along. Mother knew the man who had passed away—she always thought he had something to do with the disappearance of her chickens. We went along.

The service was held at the man's church. During the service, they asked for everyone to come and view the body. Mother and I hadn't planned to go to the funeral, but we were clean. Mother had on stockings, but no garters. There weren't pantyhose or knee-highs in those days. The stockings came just above her knees. She made some kind of knot at the top, hoping they would stay up. They didn't!! Just as she stepped to the casket, the stockings fell down. I remember that was one of the funniest things I had seen up until then.

Years later, Jimmy and I went to the funeral home to pay our respects. The mother of a neighbor had passed away. I'll call her Mrs. Doe. There were eight bodies there that day in the space for maybe four. There wasn't any family there. We had signed our names and we were getting ready to leave. Another person came in and he mumbled something. I answered what I thought he had asked. It didn't satisfy. He asked something else. I thought he asked about the lady's daughter. I answered. I had misunderstood again.

Very clearly the man said, "No. Where's Mrs. Doe?" That time, I pointed to the casket where our neighbor's mother was. He said, "NO. That's Mrs. Solid Copper. Her name is on the casket!" When told the story, the funeral home director at the time said he liked those "Mrs. Solid Coppers." About two weeks later, we went to the same funeral home to pay our respects.

Marla walked up to the casket and said, "Look, Mrs. Solid Mahogany."

Some months later, or maybe years, we had gone to town to go to the funeral home before we went back to our church for Prayer

Meeting. We were about ready to leave when a very tall, very well-endowed lady walked up to the son of the deceased. I doubt if the son was five feet tall. The lady put her arm around his shoulder and pulled him closer to her. His nose went exactly where it had no business to be. She stood there talking to him and patting him on his bald head. It was soon time for us to head to church, not only because of Marla, but her dad and mom needed to laugh also!

Five Generations

Family

Top left: Grannie with "little Hatters". Top right: Charlie and Cora Hatter with Lucy and Jimmy. Bottom Left: Jimmy and first grandchild.

Betty & Jimmy

Bottom: Jimmy and Betty led in a Valentine Banquet program in the characters of Burt Selleck (a combination of Burt Reynolds and Tom Selleck) and Dolly Diller (a combination of Dolly Parton and Phyllis Diller).

Nancy

Todd's cousins dancing at his wedding.

Elaine

Marla

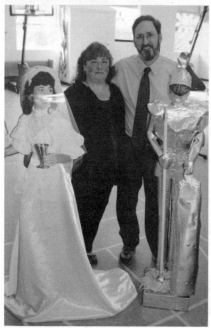

Travel

Mt. Nebo in Jordan

Seattle

Israel   Alaska

Oregon Coast   Carolina Coast

Turkey

Marla
Tidbits

When Marla started first grade, there was a piano teacher who came to the school and taught lessons. She started again in the second grade. We discovered Marla liked playing the piano, but she did not enjoy the lessons. We discontinued piano lessons until the summer after her fifth grade and began with a different teacher. The teacher became sick and could teach no longer. We changed teachers again.

After about two months, "Miss Sue" wanted to make a suggestion. Marla had the ability, but the lessons about made her sick. "Miss Sue" suggested that we keep new music in front of her at all times. After that, Marla would sit at the piano and play for at least three hours. She would play as I was cooking a meal. I enjoyed listening. This continued until she finished high school. She even played for the chorus.

After she had finished college, married and was living and working in Louisville, Marla and her best friend, Donna, were in the presence of Donna's mother, Wanda. Marla made the statement that she couldn't cook. She didn't have to; her husband cooked. Wanda preached a sermon on me about not teaching a daughter to cook. I had decided early when she was playing piano, that if she were hungry, she would learn to cook; but, in her later years she wouldn't learn how to play the piano. (Actually, Marla is a very good cook.)

For years, Wanda couldn't stand me, although she had never met me. After about twenty years, Donna was making plans to be married. Marla offered to have the reception at her home. As Marla was cleaning up after the reception, Donna told her that someone else would take care of the food. She wanted Marla to play the piano. Marla did as requested and as she played, Wanda came and sat in the chair next to the piano.

When Marla finished her first song, Wanda exclaimed, "I'll never fuss at your mother anymore." That was the first time she had heard Marla play. In the fall of 2013, Wanda's church was without a pianist. She went to the ones in charge and told them about Marla. It has really been a good match. I wrote her a thank-you note. Last year, I finally met her.

When Marla was in college, she sang in the church choir. She was also one of the twelve in a small choral group. They even did some traveling; from New Orleans to Pittsburgh. She had the opportunity to play the piano and sing for many church organizations. She played the piano for a morning session of the Kentucky Baptist Convention. Of course, I was very proud of her. She had a boyfriend, however, who didn't care for her talents. He discouraged her any way he could. Marla was home one weekend. She had plans to go to Horse Cave for an arts production with a young lawyer. She wanted something new to wear, as if he had seen all her clothes. We went to town and I bought what she wanted. (We both had to agree.)

She went back home and I stayed in town to ride home with Jimmy after he had finished the mail route. When we arrived home, the car she drove was in front of the house. She was to meet the lawyer in town. When I went inside, the new clothes we bought were in the house. I called mother to find out what she knew. Marla had called her and told her that plans had changed. I was sure the other young man had come by and messed up plans. I did a lot of walking the floor. The phone rang at ten minutes to eleven. I answered. It was the WKU student. He wanted to talk to Marla.

The conversation went like this, *"She's not here."*

"Where is she?"
"I don't know."
"Who's she with?"
"I don't know."
"When will she be back?"

"I don't know." I'm sure he thought I wasn't telling the truth. I, on the other hand, was finally at peace to go to bed and fall asleep. Marla reported in when she arrived home. Somewhere along the way, the WKU student gave Jimmy a puppy. We kept the dog, and Marla decided the young man was not for her. The young lawyer played the violin at her wedding to Michael.

OOPS

Sometimes, something very simple reminds us of an event from the past. Last week, Elaine and Ron came to my house to spend the night. Their RV had been parked in my driveway all winter, and he was going to take it home. Elaine wanted to go to our farmhouse, where she grew up, to dig some bulbs--daffodils, jonquils, or buttercups, you might call them. Jimmy had planted lots of bulbs the year before he died. She wanted some of her Dad's flowers to have in her own yard. Jimmy loved flowers. I went along with her, and while she dug up the bulbs, I picked a bunch to take home for a bouquet.

Arriving back at my house, I needed a vase to hold my flowers. I looked in the cabinet under the kitchen sink to find an appropriate container. My body was having a hard time bending over to get the vases. Elaine came to help and found the memory. We can't remember the date it happened, but we know it did. We know that I wasn't at home, but we don't remember where I was. A family member must have been sick. What Elaine had found under the sink was a partly filled box of baking soda. You may not think that baking soda is funny, but this time it was.

The phone had rung; Marla answered it. It was a neighbor calling to see if we had any baking soda. Marla told her that we did, and she would have it ready when she got to the house. Marla did have it ready for the neighbor when she arrived. The neighbor needed it to make biscuits for the night meal. She even invited Marla and Jimmy to come and eat supper with her family. When I talked with Marla on the phone, she told me the neighbor's request.

"Marla, where did you find the baking soda?" I asked.

"I knew where it was; it was on the shelf in the bathroom," she replied.

At this point, I responded, "Marla,

that baking soda was in the bathroom as a deodorizer." OOPS!

Marla in Summer of 1963

Learning to Drive

Nancy learned to drive by driving a neighbor farmer's old Ferguson tractor. If she wasn't in school, she would drive for the men to put hay, straw or tobacco on the wagon. Marla learned to drive the grain truck. She just got in and drove it from one field to another. She drives anywhere. Elaine learned to drive, driving an old car on which the reverse did not work. We lived about a half mile from the main road. She would drive the car out in the morning to catch the bus. During the school day, her dad would turn the car around and head it toward the house so that she could drive back home. Now, Elaine even drives their RV.

Bryan and Christa with Ronnie and Tammy at the farm about a year after the driving incident.

Bryan and Christa (Marla's children) came to spend a week with us. Christa, who was almost five, brought her bicycle with the training wheels. I don't remember if Bryan, who was almost seven, brought his bike. They were outside playing. I heard Bryan calling for Grannie with urgency. I went out the door and saw our straight shift Nissan coming across the road into the front yard. About the time I was outside, the car stopped at an iron pole that Jimmy had made on which to hang flower baskets. All I could see was Bryan running in front of the car and calling for me.

Where was Christa? She was driving the car. We lived off the main road and when Jimmy came home, he had parked the car and left the keys in it. When I got to Christa, she had pulled so hard on the keychain, she had torn it apart.

Christa a few years before the driving incident

I asked, "Christa, could you see over the steering wheel?" She shook her head, no. "Could you touch the brake or foot pedal?"

"No." It could have been tragic, but the worst thing that happened is that she ran over one side of the training wheels on her bike. Jimmy removed both sides of the training wheels. In less than an hour, she was riding up and down the road in front of the house like a professional. She didn't learn to drive from that experience, but she did enjoy her bike the rest of the week.

She has graduated from Western Kentucky University, has a good job, and is a very good driver.

Elaine, Betty Ruth, Marla, Nancy and Jimmy in 1964

Proud of my Girls

After Jimmy and I married, I became a part of Sulphur Spring Baptist Church. God has been good to us all of these years. God gave us three daughters Nancy, Elaine, and Marla. When Bro. David was our pastor, he would say to me, "Betty Ruth, you are always bragging on your girls." He was right. In 1984, the church celebrated 150 years, and Nancy was on the program committee. Ron was pastor of Richpond Baptist Church, and Elaine was able to be a part of the celebration. Marla was a student at Western Kentucky University and was able to be present. Bro. David and Carolyn were able to come for the weekend. Bro. David came to me and said, "Betty Ruth, you have every reason to brag on your girls." I have always tried to be an encourager to my girls and all of the other youth at church.

Flowers and Cardinals

Jimmy and I liked flowers, he was the one who had to look after them because of the bees and other insects that didn't agree with me. Sometimes when he came in from the mail route, he would take care of the flowers before he would come into the house and see about me.

We always liked birds, especially male cardinals. Their colors were beautiful. Jimmy fed them, and they liked our deck and the peach tree beside it. After our corn was picked, there were always leftovers. Jimmy would go through the field and pick up the ears that had been left. He had made a way for the ears of corn to be placed on the deck rail, and the cardinals would have a feast.

I always heard that blue jays were mean birds, but that was not the case at our house. When the cardinal could not remove the grain of corn from the cob, the bluejay would come to the deck and remove seven or eight grains and go on their way. The bluejays didn't eat the corn, but they helped the cardinals. On one occasion, when I wasn't at home, Jimmy counted forty-four male cardinals on the deck rail and in the peach tree. What a beautiful sight God provided.

Ron, Betty Ruth, Jimmy and Matt at a
Campbellsville College football game

Snow Fun

Ronnie, our grandson, played for the
Campbellsville University football team. We
tried to go to all of his games. Jimmy, Ron,
Elaine, Matthew, Mother and I were on our
way to Jackson, Tennessee for Ronnie's
game. We were on Interstate 40 between
Nashville and Dickson when it began to
snow. There was a rest area in Dickson,
and we decided we should make a pit stop
before we went along the way. The men were
the first outside, where Jimmy and Matthew
started playing in the snow. Matthew made
a snow ball, and was ready to throw it at
his Pappaw. Jimmy lined himself up in front
of Mother. Just at the right time, Matthew
threw, Pappaw ducked and Mother was hit

with the snowball. Matthew thought he was going to be in trouble. Thankfully, his great-grandmother was forgiving. We went on our way with no hard feelings. That was all of the snow that day.

Chain Saw

During my younger years, I had migraine headaches. In the early eighties, I was curled up on the couch, when all of a sudden the chain saw started in the basement. I didn't try to get off the couch, and it is good thing that I didn't. Almost immediately, the chain saw blade came through the floor. I could have lost a leg or maybe both. My husband came upstairs to see how things had gone. He was positive he had told me what he was doing. Besides cutting through the floor, he had cut a brand new carpet that had been laid three weeks earlier. He accomplished what he had intended to do and it worked. Son-in-law, Michael, wishes he could have been there. He still thinks it is funny. In my opinion, a running chainsaw and a migraine headache do not "mix."

The Worst Gift Ever

(Marla wanted me to include this story.)

I don't remember the year, but for my birthday, January 11th, or our anniversary, January 29th, my husband gave me a gift he was very happy about. When I opened the package, it was a GIRDLE. Not just any girdle, it was SIZES too large. I started to cry.

Jimmy said, "You said you needed one."

"The girdle," I said, "was bad enough, but what about the size?"

His reply was, "I held it up, and it looked as if it would fit." That didn't help. Six months later, he asked, "What did you do with the girdle I gave you?"

I told him, "I wrapped it in tissue paper

and put it away. I told the girls where it is, and they are to give it to your next wife." Of course, that is never going to happen, but it made me feel better at the time. It's still put away. I hope I don't grow into it.

One Liners

Our Sunday school lesson was about being first beside Jesus. I asked the 3rd and 4th grade boys and girls to tell me someplace they would like to be first in line. Without breathing, a farmer's son spoke up, "I WANT TO BE FIRST IN LINE AT HUDSON'S GRAIN BINS." That was the most honest answer I ever received. He had waited many times for two or more hours in a hot truck for wheat, corn, or soybeans to be unloaded.

Our church was electing deacons on a Sunday morning. I was trying to tell the 3rd and 4th graders about some of the jobs these elected people would do. I asked, "What do you call these people?" Everything was quiet, and finally one girl spoke up and said, "DEMONS."

Marla:

Nancy made most of Marla's clothes when Marla was very young. She would make something for herself and take the material that was left over and sew for Marla. One Sunday, Marla had on a new dress. An older, larger lady asked Marla if Nancy would make her a new dress. Marla answered, "No, she doesn't have enough material."

Eric:

Eric enjoyed telling me, "Grannie, you are the same age as the speed limit—a five and a five". That was also a few years ago.

Christa:

Christa was learning the names of all the presidents. I told her I had to learn the presidents when I was in school. "YES," she replied, but "GRANNIE, YOU DIDN'T HAVE AS MANY TO LEARN BACK THEN".

Matthew:

Matthew wanted a peanut butter and jelly sandwich. I started getting it ready for him. I put the peanut butter on one slice of bread and the jelly on the other. Matthew was upset and said, "GRANNIE, YOU PUT THE PEANUT BUTTER ON THE WRONG SLICE OF BREAD." I quickly put the two pieces together and said, "IT'S ON THE RIGHT ONE NOW."

Jimmy always changed the oil in the cars and tractor. He would save the oil for use for something else. He would always think that he had put it out of the way. When Ronnie and Jameson would come to our house, they proved him wrong. They would have fun, but what a mess to get them cleaned up! Matthew wasn't old enough to enjoy the mess.

Mr. Jess:
Mr. Jess was our neighbor on the farm. He was a twin and he had never married. He could make the best popcorn anyone ever ate. Somehow, Mr. Jess heard that Jimmy gave me a clothes dryer for my birthday, so he came to visit and see it. When he asked where it was, it was full of clothes in front of the grate to dry. When he realized that it was

not an electric clothes dryer, he wasn't very happy. He had told several people about the gift that Jimmy had given me.

Grandma:

Most of the time, I drove Jimmy's mom to the doctor. On one occasion, the doctor discussed some problem and then asked if she had any pain. She slowly nodded her head.

"Where?" asked the doctor. She touched her left arm and then her right leg.

"SOMETIMES IT'S HERE AND SOMETIMES IT'S THERE". I laughed. It was funny, but laughter is catching. I'm about the age she was then, and I have some of those sometimes here and sometimes there pains.

One Sunday afternoon, Jameson could not be found, and his brothers didn't know where he was. The family called the Bowling Green Police Department, and neighbors started helping look for him. Ron was pastor of a church a few miles out of Bowling Green. Finally, a member of the church called to tell them that she had Jameson with her. He was walking on his way to church. Ron and Elaine wanted to know why he was running away from home.

He answered, "I wasn't running away from home. I was running away from homework." That fourth grader has been deployed to Iraq twice. He is now a Chaplain, with a rank of Captain, in the US Army.

Christa's words of wisdom:
"You know you are an adult when your toothbrush falls into the commode and YOU are the one who has to retrieve it."

The congregation was singing, "Sweet, Sweet Spirit." The pastor's wife was seated on the second pew from the front, holding her misbehaving young son. As we sang the line, "there are sweet expressions on each face," the pastor's wife went by the piano carrying her son under her right arm. He was kicking and hollering, then pleading, "DON'T PULL MY PANTS DOWN!" There was not a sweet expression on either of their faces.

Jameson's graduation from Officer Candidate School

A Long Trip

Jameson graduated last month from Chaplain school. July 20th, the army sends him to Fort Lewis, Washington. He will serve the army as a pastor. His congregation will be soldiers and their families. He will be known as Chaplain Williams. Leaving South Carolina to go to Washington State, their minivan was crowded. There was his family--Heather, Jay, Hailey, Parker and Jameson-- pack and play, clothes for very hot days as well as cold days, Jameson's military gear, toys, etc.

The second day of their fourteen day trip, they stopped at my house to spend the night. As they traveled, they stopped to enjoy the things God made. The last day of traveling was a long day. As they prepared to

arrive at Fort Lewis, Parker, who had his third birthday the day before, spoke up.

"I TIRED OF THIS CAR, MAY I PLEASE BE EXCUSED?" It wouldn't have been safe to let him out of his car seat, and it would have been against the law. It would not be safe to open the door and push him out, so I'm sorry to say Parker could not "be excused."

At the time of this writing, it's April, 2015. In June, they will be traveling to Fort Hood, Texas. May God continue to bless them, and may they always be able to help others.

Pool Party

I didn't plan this party, but I changed the atmosphere. There was a swimming party planned for the whole church. I probably wouldn't have gone. My mother always said, "Never go near the water until you learn how to swim." One week and a half before the party, they announced the oldest one there wearing a bathing suit would be recognized. It was Sunday morning worship time, but my brain took off.

When I arrived home, I called Elaine and asked if she could find me an old-fashioned bathing suit on the internet. She called back and let me know that she had found one. I went to the Arts Council the very next day to see if they had a suit, but they didn't. So,

Elaine ordered one for me. FedEx delivered it just in time for me to do a little remodeling. I had only told one other person what I had planned and asked her to help me.

Time came. Pizza was served. I had worn my regular clothes. Laura Benton came to watch the restroom door and help in any way. After I changed clothes, she took pictures. We emerged into the crowd. The children thought I was dressed for Halloween in August. The adults loved it. The person that had planned the night thanked me. She said I always knew how to liven up a party. By the way, the tag on the bathing suit said, "Dry Clean Only!

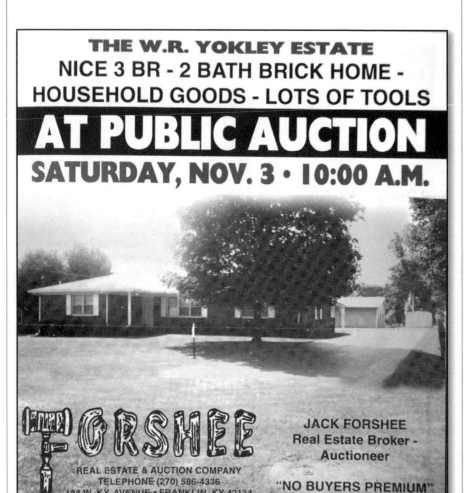

Last Four Months

Jimmy and I bought a house in town on the third of November, 2001. I don't know why we did. We just had a new $6000 roof put on the farmhouse. The house had a twenty-eight by forty foot workshop. I said at the time, "we bought the workshop, and the house came with it."

We got possession of the town house on November 9th and then left town Nov. 12th. We were going to North Carolina and then Fort Benning with Elaine and Ron for their second son's graduation from basic training. We stayed over Thanksgiving and went to church with Elaine and Ron on Sunday. After coming home, we spent one night and then went to Louisville to see Marla's children in

Christmas programs at school and church. We were there a week and we decided on the way home that we wouldn't do anything to the house in town until after the first of the new year.

February 16, 2002 at Cumberland College the day before Jimmy died.

The Last Weekend-- On February 15, 2002, we left home to go to eastern Kentucky and meet Elaine, Ron, their son and his family. Ronnie was assistant coach for the girls' basketball team of Georgetown College in Kentucky. We were going to the basketball game between Georgetown College and Cumberland College.

We had the best time. We ate breakfast together, and Ronnie left to help with the team. We watched the game, and then decided we would start home while it was still daylight. When we stopped at a restaurant in Glasgow, Ky to eat, Jimmy witnessed to our waiter, as he did anywhere we went. We arrived home about 9:00 pm.

After our night's rest, we prepared for church. They were having breakfast that Sunday morning. Time came, Jimmy went to his class and I went to mine. When Sunday School was over, our choir director told us we were not having choir. I found a place to sit and Jimmy came in and sat beside me, not his usual place to sit. Church service began and they called on Jimmy to lead in prayer. He prayed, we sang a song, and we sat down.

Something else started, and I was watching. I heard Jimmy make an unusual noise, I heard it again. By that time, our family doctor was coming to him. He recognized the sound. Dr. Mike was just across the aisle, not his usual place to sit. A paramedic was at church "on call" with the ambulance and all the equipment outside the church door. There was a registered nurse, many that could give CPR and all of them loved Jimmy.

With all the prayers and help, Jimmy didn't make it – no known heart problem. His last spoken word was "AMEN." I've never had to say, "if only." God took care of all that. Oh, I still miss him. We were married fifty-three years. Now, I know why we bought the house in town. My mother was still living, and she would not have let me stay in the country house. God prepared a place for me before I knew I needed it.

*Painting of Sulphur Spring Baptist Church
by Jameson Williams*

Testimony

Before Christmas 2014, I was looking for something special. I found something I didn't expect to find. I found our church bulletin dated March 16, 2003. As I looked more closely at the morning's service, there was my name to give a testimony. Included in the bulletin were the notes I had written for that testimony. I thought, "why not include them in what I am writing".

So, here it is:
Some of you have said to me, "Betty Ruth, there's always something going on in your life." That's right, there is. These last two years, my life has been a giant roller coaster ride. There have been the ups, and there have been the downs.

Two years ago today, Nancy was in Bowling Green Medical Center. I couldn't have imagined that, three days later, Nancy would no longer be with us. You gave us comfort. I leaned on Jimmy, and together we leaned on the Lord. Life went on with its ups and downs.

The first of October, a wasp stung me on the hand! Jimmy told Elaine and Marla that he thought he had lost me. About the middle of October, Jimmy and I were leaving town. He drove to Westview Heights. He knew of a house that could be for sale. He also remembered that the house had a workshop. We drove around the block six times. November 3, 2001, we bought the workshop and the house came with it.

My roller coaster life hit its lowest point, February 17, 2002. Philippians 4:19 says, "My God shall supply all your need according to his riches in glory by Christ Jesus." God has supplied my need. He has used YOU, my church family. God was here that day. Usually, I would have been in the choir; Jimmy would have gone behind the back pew and he would have sat down somewhere on the small aisle. Instead, we were in the center. Dr. Mike was across the aisle—not his normal seat. Stacy was on call and was here with the emergency equipment outside—that happens one out of every four Sundays. There was a registered nurse in the congregation. God had other plans. God gave a peace; Philippians 4:7 says it is "a peace that passes all understanding." God used you to take care of me when I couldn't take care of myself. All of you gave comfort.

I couldn't have stayed on the farm by myself with the wasps and other insects that like to eat me and I don't like snakes. It wouldn't have been safe. God already provided the house in town even before we knew I needed it. Some of you helped get the house ready. Some of you moved furniture—even the piano. I haven't spent another night at the farm even up to now.

I have come to some of you for advice -- "Do I sell my grain or store it?", "What about insurance?", "What about my car?" There have been other questions. I came to some of you for a shoulder to cry on. God has used some of you to come to me and offer a shoulder. You seem to know when I have a need. You give me a hug, maybe you say something, maybe you don't. You ask me to your home or out to eat. You've sent flowers, there's a telephone call, or a note in the mailbox. You knocked on my door when it snowed to see if there was a need. God sent you to my door where you knew there was a need. You prayed for me.

One of my biggest concerns was my driving or not driving. Again, God has used you to provide my need. You see that I get to church on Wednesday evenings and back home after choir practice. If the weather is bad on Sunday mornings, you call and say, "We'll be there for you." You've given me rides to recitals, graduations, etc. I could go on.

I heard Ron preach last May, 2002. He was telling what the Greek word was for: "to boost, to lift up." Remembering that I was there, he added an illustration. When we went to Israel and Jordan, I needed to ride a horse. It was Ron's job to give me a boost. When we arrived home and shared about the event, someone asked if he took a picture. He said, "No. From where he was standing, it was not a pretty sight." Thank you for the boost, and I'm sure it hasn't been a pretty sight. I am amazed and very thankful for the people God has used to supply my need.

Last year (2002), I went to Dr. Mike's office. I sat down by a lady that I sort of knew. She was forty-nine years old and had lost her husband about a month before Jimmy's death. As we talked about our circumstances, she said to me, "My faith has been shattered." I answered her, "My faith is stronger."

Philippians 4:19 says, "My God shall supply all your needs according to his riches in glory by Christ Jesus." And, HE HAS. Philippians 4:20 – "Now unto God our Father be glory forever and ever. AMEN."

Even though this was written in March 2003, my church family is still meeting my needs in January 2015.

Even at Piggly Wiggly

A few weeks ago, I went to Piggly Wiggly to get some groceries. When I reached the check-out, before the lady started checking me out, she said, "I want to ask you to do something for me. I wouldn't ask just anyone, but you seem to be a fine Christian woman. Will you pray for me and my family?" Something very sad had happened in her family. I promised her that I would. I not only prayed that day but several days that followed.

The words, "you seem like a fine Christian woman" kept ringing in my head. I did not know the woman's name and the only place I had ever seen her was at Piggly Wiggly. She only knew my name on my check when I paid for groceries. I know God sees everything I do, but what had she seen?

Before I went to the country of Greece, she asked me to bring her a postcard. I took her a postcard that I had chosen for her. Hopefully, that demonstrated to her that I tried to keep my word.

There was a day that I had been to Piggly Wiggly and I only bought four things. When I arrived home, I realized that they hadn't charged me for one of the items I bought. It was less than two dollars, but after I put away what I bought, I went back to Piggly Wiggly to give them the money I owed. Maybe she was at the next check-out and knew that I tried to be honest.

I try to say, "please" and, "thank you" when I should. She has not heard me say bad words.

In the Bible, in Proverbs 20:11, it says, *"Even a child is known by his doings, whether they be good and pure."* God is watching you too, but there are others. You are being watched at home. Some of you have younger brothers and sisters. They watch everything you do, and then they want to try it. People are watching you at church. They are watching you at school. Then, there is Walmart and McDonald's.

I still don't know what the lady saw in me, but I do know that people are watching us, even at Piggly Wiggly.

Betty Ruth sharing a children's sermon at
Sulphur Spring Baptist Church

Children's Sermon

Peter and John went to the Temple one afternoon to take part in the three o'clock prayer meeting. As they approached the Temple, they saw a man being carried and laid down by the Gate called Beautiful. This man had never been able to walk in all his life. Family or friends carried him each day to the gate for him to ask for money.

As Peter and John were passing by, the man asked them for money. Peter told the man to look into his eyes. The man did as Peter asked because he was expecting money.

Peter said, "We don't have any money for you, but I give you what I have. In the name of Jesus Christ of Nazareth, rise up and walk." Then Peter took the lame man by the right hand and lifted him up. He began walking and jumping and praising God. He even went to the Temple with Peter and John. People around saw what happened. They knew it was the same man who had never been able to walk who was now jumping and walking. They were amazed.

In those days, if someone in this situation asked you for money, you were supposed to give. Peter and John didn't have any money, but in the name of Jesus Christ, they gave him something much better. They said they would give the man what they could.

I believe each one of us have been given abilities to use for God's work. In our church recently, they asked for some people to drive the church bus. We're not all given the same talents. That is one that I didn't get, but I think there are those in the church that have the talent of church bus driving.

Sometimes our abilities change. There was a time I was known for frying chicken. I don't fry much chicken any more. We try to eat healthier. We a had a pastor and his family leave our church for Argentina and the mission field. When they came back to the states on furlough, they came to church and we had a potluck meal. Their middle child was about nine years old when they left. Then, four years later she walked up to the food table. There were twelve to fifteen platters of fried chicken on the table. She looked for just a little bit and then said, "Miss Betty Ruth, this is your chicken." She was right. Instead of fried chicken, now days I'm asked if I will make a Honey Bun cake.

You are beginning to develop your abilities. Some of you play sports like football, basketball, baseball or others. Some of you are on the sign team, you sing, some cook and so much more.

There are at least three things that each one of you can do now. Each of you can smile. When you **smile** at someone, most of the time, they will smile back. You can **speak kind words**. You can **pray** for others.

Like Peter and John, most of us would have to say "Silver and gold have I none." We don't have the money, but we do have talents we can use in Jesus' name.

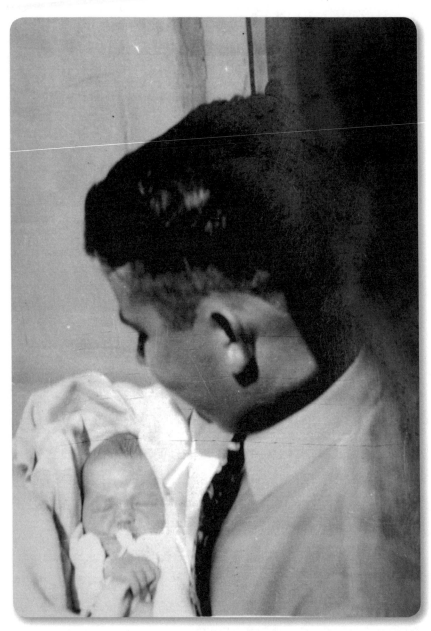

Jimmy holding Nancy

God's Goodness

I have always tried to be an encourager. Seven years ago I went to the high school to talk about a scholarship in Dr. Nancy E. Hatter's memory. The corn crop brought more than usual. I decided I could put $5000 in a scholarship fund and give $1000 a year. Surely there would be another good crop year before the five years were gone. I have been able to replace the $1000 each year. I have given seven scholarships in the six years. I know that a thousand dollars is not a lot, but it does let a student know that someone cares.

If you could see my bank account, you would probably say that I couldn't afford it. Jimmy gave the hospital a cold check for me to get into the hospital before Nancy was born. The check was only $50, but there wasn't $50 in the bank. There was a small check at home. He was able to put it in the bank early Monday morning so we would not be overdrawn.

God has been good to us. I don't choose the student, but it makes me feel so good to present a check in Nancy's memory. The first one to receive a scholarship hopes to be a pediatric doctor in Africa. Three other recipients, two young men and one young woman, are also preparing for the mission field. One young man is studying to be a veterinarian, and another is in the field of engineering. I am constantly amazed at God's provision and His continued goodness, even as I see Him working in young people.

Life Changes

Life changed for us with Nancy's death in 2001. It changed again in 2002 with Jimmy's death. It started changing again in 2011. Elaine and Ron were living in Boiling Springs, North Carolina. Ron was now "Dr. Ron," as he had earned his PhD and been teaching at Gardner Webb University for over sixteen years.

We knew that Ron needed surgery on his spine, and I had gone home with them to stay with Ron, so that Elaine would be free to work at the school. During his surgery, the doctor nicked his spinal column. So, he had another surgery. Another complication arose causing Ron to have a seizure and a stroke-like event. Between the two surgeries, I was at home making peanut butter fudge, and it was about ready. I wasn't feeling well, so I turned off the heat and pushed the pan to the back of the stove. That was all I remember. When I came to, I was on the floor facing the other direction. It turned out, I had broken my right ankle. Now, Elaine had two patients!

What was I Thinking?

People have asked me if I was thinking about Nancy and Jimmy's death in the title. No! I really had my own life and death experience on my mind. Nancy and Jimmy's deaths were both very sad, but each time God also gave blessings. I know that Nancy has gone to live in Heaven. She now has renewed health, and she feels loved. God didn't leave any "if onlys" with Jimmy's death. How many people can say that "Amen" was their last spoken word? Everything was done for him that could have been done, and trained people were by his side quicker than if he had been in a hospital.

It's still amazing to me to see how God worked so that I would be taken care of. The house in town is still a miracle. Jimmy and I had worked on that house after buying it. The three bedrooms were ready for us to occupy. Very little had to be done that afternoon for the house to be slept in. Dr. Mike cooked the first meal in that kitchen. Our pastor's young daughters vacuumed the carpets.

Todd and Eric, our grandsons, went out to the farmhouse and brought the couch and chair from the living room, the kitchen table and chairs and a few other things. They stopped at the church and brought my car to town. Todd remembered seeing my medicine back at the farmhouse and asked if he needed to go back and bring it to town. I was very thankful because I had not even thought of it.

It was late in the afternoon when Marla was finally able to contact Elaine and Ron. They lived about eight hours away. Around eleven, they called to say that they needed to stop for the night, and they would arrive in the morning. On Monday morning Marla, Todd, Eric, Jody (Todd and Eric's Uncle) and I moved a few more things. God took care of me again. I am able to call this house my home.

Betty Ruth arrived in Oregon, her 50th state!

Life
Continued

After my heart stopped, they packed me in plastic bags of ice. The friend I'd called earlier returned my call, and the EMT answered my phone. After hearing the news, my friend hurried to the hospital and then called the girls. They say my heart stopped a second and a third time. The nurse came and told my friend that they couldn't bring me back a fourth time. He was to tell Elaine and Marla not to go to Vanderbilt but to come on to Franklin. About twenty minutes later, they came back and told my friend to call the girls. They decided to work with me and I finally responded. The helicopter they called was on its way from Vanderbilt. I had four stints put in. They didn't think I'd make it...but I did. They called me a walking miracle.

After a week, I was sent to a rehab center. Close to the end of my ten day stay, my shoulder was in constant pain; so the doctor prescribed some medicine and they sent me home. My son-in-law, Michael, came to take care of me, but he could tell I wasn't reacting well. So, he put me in the car and drove me straight to the emergency room. He says I talked about strange things like "where the nest was" when we were pulling into the ER parking lot.

The doctors thought I had a stroke and soon decided to send me back to Vanderbilt. They called for the helicopter, and I knew when they put me in, but I never knew when we landed. I was unconscious. The doctors couldn't decide what the trouble was. Michael and my grandson, Ronnie, offered the suggestion that I might be allergic to some medicines. They were right. I should never have had the pain medicine they gave me in rehab. After correcting my medication, I was soon in my right mind again. Michael stayed with me for seven weeks. He cooked (He is a great cook.), cleaned, did laundry, drove me to the doctor and never let me get out of a chair unless he was helping me.

Later in the summer of 2012, doctors gave permission for Ron and I to travel by airplane. We already had our tickets. We were flying to the Seattle-Tacoma airport. Elaine and Ron's chaplain son was stationed in Ft. Lewis. We had not yet had the opportunity to visit with them at that location. I also had another opportunity. I had visited forty-nine states. This was a chance to visit Oregon, my fiftieth state. We did it! I had dreamed of visiting all fifty states, and this trip fulfilled that dream.

Now What?

Since 2012, after my heart problems, there have been many new opportunities:

*I have taken a trip to Oregon.

*I have been able to see my dear friend earn his Bachelor's Degree at age forty-three.

*I was Grannie in the children's Christmas program. I wore my pajamas just as the children did.

*Elaine and Ron moved from Boiling Springs, North Carolina to Owensboro, Kentucky. They moved because of his health, but it has since improved. He taught two classes at Owensboro Community College, fall of 2015. He is now interim pastor at the church where they are now members.

*Elaine was elected deacon at the church where they moved their membership. I hoped to be there for the ordination service on November 1, 2015, so my dear friend and his wife drove me to the ordination service. God allowed me to see my daughter ordained, and I was a proud momma.

*I have observed that Elaine was also named to their pastor search committee.

*I watched my three-year-old great-grandson ride a skateboard (without a skateboard, which was very interesting).

*The Sunday before Thanksgiving 2015, I saw my great-grandson, Kindrick baptized.

*In January 2016, Ron, Elaine and I flew to Dallas and on to Fort Hood. We visited Jameson and his family for a week. Great-granddaughter, eleven-year-old Hailey, made a cake and a card for my birthday on that first day.
*I've enjoyed watching some of my great-grandchildren's school activities: baseball, softball, basketball, concerts, instrument recitals and singing.

*I've met new friends.

*Each day God provides some new blessing. If my heart had not started again, there would not have been the added enjoyment I have experienced. God would have blessed some other way.

Tomorrow is just a day away. We don't know what it might bring. Put your trust in Jesus Christ and serve Him. Maybe you need to put into print some of your own memories. Three of my memories that I have passed ·down are almost one-hundred years old. They may be old, but they are all still funny.

May God Bless You!!!

FAMILY

I never thought my family would look like this:

Jimmy – attended farm school after the army
Nancy – Doctor of Early Childhood Education
Ron – PhD and University Professor
Elaine – Master's Degree in School Counseling
Marla – Bachelor of Computer Science with additional hours.
Michael – Master's in Special Education – teacher of social studies, special needs students, and football coach
Ronnie – Master's in Education and Special Education, Rank I, high school principal, women's basketball coach for college teams for ten plus years, boys' basketball coach
Tammy – Master's in Physical Therapy, additional certifications
Jameson –Master of Divinity, working on D.Min., chaplain; Captain,U.S. Army
Heather—Bachelor degree in Social Work, home school teacher and great support for Jameson
Matthew – Master's in Business Administration. He and his mom received their masters' the same day from the same university.
Shannon – Bachelor's in Family Living and Child Development, preschool teacher
Todd – took classes at Technical School. He is one of the hardest workers I have ever seen.
Eric – They say that Eric can fix anything. He and Todd, along with their uncle, farm MANY acres of land.
Bryan – almost through with a Bachelor's Degree
Christa – Bachelor's in Communications. Has a good job.

Then, there is **ME**. I have a High School Diploma. I even know where it is after sixty-seven years.

Watercolor painting of the farm house by Jameson Williams

*Betty Ruth ready for church a few short
months after her heart attack*

Grannie with nine of the great-grandchildren

The Swimsuit